T0161114

HORIZONS

POEMS OF
LIFE AND LOVE

KATHRYN CAROLE ELLISON

Published by Lady Bug Books, an imprint of Brisance Books Group.
Lady Bug Press and the distinctive ladybug logo are registered trademarks of
Lady Bug Books, LLC.

Lady Bug Books
400 112th Avenue N.E.
Suite 230
Bellevue, WA 98004
www.GiftsOfLove.com

For information about custom editions, special sales and permissions, please email
Info@GiftsOfLove.com

Manufactured in the United States of America
ISBN: 978-1-944194-70-3

First Edition: September 2020

A NOTE FROM THE AUTHOR

The poems in this book were written over many years as gifts to my children. I began writing them in the 1970s, when they were reaching the age of reason. And, as I found myself in the position of becoming a single parent, I wanted to do something special to share with them—something that would become a tradition, a ritual they could count on.

And so the Advent Poems began—one day, decades ago—with a poem 'gifted' to them each day during the Advent period leading up to Christmas, December 1 to December 24. Forty some years later... my children still look forward each year to the poems that started a family tradition, that new generations have come to cherish.

It is my sincere hope that you will embrace and enjoy them, and share them with those you love.

Children of the Light was among the early poems I wrote, and is included in each of the *Poems of Life and Love* books in The Ellison Collection: *Heartstrings, Celebrations, Inspirations, Sanctuary, Awakenings, Sojourns, Milestones, Tapestry, Gratitude, Beginnings, Horizons* and *Moments*. After writing many hundreds of poems, it is still my favorite. The words came from my heart... and my soul... and flowed so effortlessly that it was written in a single sitting.
All I needed to do was capture the words on paper.

Light, to me, represented all that was good and pure and right with the world, and I believed then—as I do today—that those elements live in my children, and perhaps in all of us.
We need only to dare.

– KCE

DEDICATION

To my parents: Herb and Bernice Haas

Mom, you were the poet who went before me...
unpublished, but appreciated nonetheless.

And Dad, you always believed in me,
no matter what direction my life took.
Thank you for your faith in me,
and for your unconditional love.

TABLE OF CONTENTS

LIFE'S JOYS

LIFE'S LESSONS

LIFE'S GIFTS

LIFE'S JOYS

CHOOSE YOUR OWN PATH

It may sound easy just to accept
Another's ideas and influence.
But is it really? Stop and think!!
It might have a terrible consequence.

And if your attitude is one of apathy –
("What difference does it make, anyway?")
You'll spend your whole lifetime on the sidelines,
And never find your own true way.

You don't have to just mindlessly travel along
A life chain which you've inherited.
You are worth the effort to expand yourself.
It's an obligation which you have merited.

You have the right to choose your own path
And the people who'll help along the way –
With treatments that have the most benefit for you;
So start now, without delay.

Put yourself in the position of number one –
Item A, Top of the List, First Place –
Of those who will determine the paths you'll take;
And the highest and best you'll embrace.

CHILDREN OF THE LIGHT

There are those souls who bring the light,
Who spill it out for all to share.
And with a joy that does excite,
They show the world that they do care.
It is so very bright.

In this sharing, love does pervade
Into their lives and cycles round;
And as this light is outward played
The love is also inward bound.
It is an awesome trade.

You are a soul whose light is shared.
It comes from deep within your heart.
It's best because it is not spared,
Because it's total, not just part.
And I am glad you've dared.

FREE

The image that comes to mind of ideal childhood
Is one of waving grass high on a hill –
Of laughter uncontrolled that wafts so lightly –
And running through tall grass to take a spill.

Looking up at clouds when lying down,
I'm counting all the angels and the sheep.
The grass is tickling my bare arms and legs,
But that's okay – I'm nearly fast asleep.

And when I wake I hear the bubbling brook
That began in the mountains far from here;
And grazing near its gentle banks I see
A herd of doe-eyed white-tailed deer.

What comes to mind for you of ideal childhood?
We've heard enough of what I'd like to see.
I wish for you a million joys in your lifetime,
And may your heart's child remain forever free.

ETERNITY

Eternity is not endless time,
And it is not the opposite of time.
It is actually the essence of time.

If you quickly spin a wheel of color
They all blend to make a single color.
White is the essence of color.

If you quickly spin the wheel of time –
Past, present, and future blend of time –
Eternity is the essence of time.

Sometimes an event occurs in our lives —
Perhaps a beautiful time in our lives,
Or even a painful event in our lives;

Then we catch a glimpse at that special time
Of eternity that is 'all time' —
Of what our lives are about all the time.

We stand on the threshold of eternity.
All times a-spin is eternity.
The essence of time is eternity.

LETTING GO

Letting go seems to be a most difficult task,
But it's important for growth and evolution.
When you let go, you become part of everything.
You're no longer the problem, but the solution.

You are part of all you have met – so am I –
And all of which you'll ever see.
I saw people approaching, but all were the same.
They were all no one but me.

If you want to know me, look inside yourself,
Because that's where I'll dwell forever.
Think of the whole being greater than the sum
Of the parts, and you'll be very clever.

BELIEVE IN YOURSELF

Your thoughts precede your actions every time,
Which span from 'most ridiculous' to sublime.
The positive ones can guarantee success,
No matter the extent of your duress.
The negative ones bring fear and doubts galore
And take away your courage to explore.

Believe in Yourself! (It's bold advice!)
It's most important to see yourself as 'High Price!'
You are the best you in the world, by far.
(Compared to others, you measure well above par.)
A habit of confidence makes you rule supreme,
Allowing for pursuit of your every dream.

You can criticize or be congratulating –
(Your motives you are ever articulating.)
Success lies always well within your rule.
Accept responsibility for its schedule.
There's nothing in the world you can't achieve
As long as in yourself you do believe.

PEACE

To find yourself you must lose yourself.
(Read on – it's your path to recovery.)
Your doubts and worries and inhibitions
Block your path to self-discovery.

Your journey through life is to discover yourself,
To test the very mettle of your soul.
When climbing a mountain with all its dangers,
You must focus on survival, as a whole.

Remain strong, and be creative, as you tread your path,
Solving each problem as it presents;
Breaking through the limitations you've placed on yourself,
Reaching beyond to your very essence.

The mountain you've climbed is the mountain of self.
The obstacles? The limitations which smother.
Your breaking through to self discovery happens
By focusing energy outward to others.

The way of all peace? Scale the mountain of self.
Overcome self-imposed obstacles as they rise.
Get out of yourself, and find yourself,
And be confidently and peacefully wise.

SIMPLICITY OF NATURE

Nature! Look at it! It's all out there,
Waiting for your participation!
And what calls you there in a very loud voice?
Universal urges... you're part of the congregation!

It's true! Nature is created by the same source
That created mankind and all things.
We're made up of the same chemicals as all of nature!
That's stardust, remember? The heart sings!

The fantasy of communing with nature, it seems,
Includes mountains and forests and islands and streams.
They're inspiring images, these natural settings.
So, make reality from those dreams!

Trek or ski, or camp in the woods.
Swim in the ocean, or river or lake.
Ride horseback through trails, or sit by a campfire.
You'll experience joy and peace, whatever choice you make.

LOOKING — OR SEEING

"Looking" and "seeing" use two different sets
Of equipment you have within.
"Looking" and "seeing" are but qualities of
Your experience, or where you have been.

Some people respond, "I see," when they mean
"I have not the foggiest notion..."
And some see beyond words to the depths of their souls,
To the bottom of the deepest ocean.

You can teach yourself to look in depth
In order to watch your life unfold.
Never turn your back on reality, my dears;
It surrounds you. It's there to behold.

When you think you can "see," look again and again.
Don't hesitate. Don't blink. Look again.
What you see may not be what you thought it was,
But be grateful for the knowledge you attain.

SUNLIGHT

No matter how dark the night, the sun rises
And chases all the shadows away.
The sun rose today; it will do it tomorrow.
The sun comes up every day.

The mornings are full of sunshine and hope...
It's a wonderful time to start over again –
Whether a continuation of yesterday's project
Or a new one you're about to begin.

A little coffee, a little sunlight...
Your troubles will begin to fade.
By focusing on your hopes and dreams
You'll turn lemons into lemonade.

Happiness can be found in the darkest of times.
Turn your own light on without delay.
Worry does not keep it from raining tomorrow;
It keeps it from being sunny today.

What sunshine gives to the flowers that bloom,
Smiles are the same gifts to humanity.
The good that smiles do, however trifling it seems,
May lead humankind back to sanity.

A flower cannot live without sunshine;
You cannot thrive without love and a dream.
Learn from the flowers which angle towards the sun...
Lean toward people you hold in high esteem.

The sun rises, the sun falls, the wind blows, the birds sing.
No matter who you are, the story is the same.
These experiences unite us all around the world –
Togetherness in friendship is good, I proclaim!

IMAGINATION

You reach into the heavens to grasp an idea,
Then you bring it to earth to make it work.
"Imagination," says Einstein, "is more powerful than knowledge."
Behind your minds the art does lurk.

Imagination enlarges vision; it challenges the impossible.
Without it the mind's barely alive.
It's awakened anew by curiosity and discontent,
And ignited by your senses, all five.

You use your imagination to examine what you see
With fresh eyes, as from the cave into the light.
You rub shoulders with people to create new sparks
That generate new concepts, and new sight.

The great master, Thomas Edison, when asked about invention,
Said simply, "I listen from within."
Imagination is a beacon in a magic lamp.
It's vital. It's powerful, and genuine.

You recognize the facts, then imagination digs deeper,
To allow for problem solving at its peak.
Imagination stirs up the Infinity in us,
And helps us find the answers that we seek.

SELF AWARENESS

Montaigne said it succinctly: "The greatest thing in the world
Is to know how to belong to one's self." (It's a gift.)
The curious paradox: when you accept yourself
Just as you are, you can change. (Make a shift.)

It doesn't matter who you love, or where you live,
You take yourself with you everywhere.
If you don't know who you are, or if you've forgotten,
You'll feel you don't belong – anywhere.

Emerson stated: "If I've lost confidence in myself
I have the universe against me."
You are perfect as you are, and you could use a little work.
Keep striving to be better. Be what you seem to be.

Your life is a novel. Every day is a page.
And you are the author in charge.
You have the power to make the story beautiful.
Make it go the way you want, small or large.

Self-awareness is important if you want to move on
In your life – in a positive manner.
If you notice a destructive pattern emerging
Chances are it's with you, and not with another.

Being in tune with your weakness puts you
In greater tune with your strengths.
At the center of your being you will discover yourself,
Realizing your purpose. (Go to great lengths.)

BELIEVING IS SEEING

To understand all that there is to know
Before you enter into life's whole plan –
To ask for it tied neatly with a bow
Is asking for a lot in one life span.
You need not understand more than you can.
You're woven into a very complex pattern.
It's a bigger picture – bigger than one man.
In one lifetime it would be hard to learn.
Believing in the unseen eases the mind's churn.

A sense of faith – it's also known as trust –
In the design of which you are a part
Will bring you comfort as we have discussed;
Will ease the yearnings of a heavy heart.
To navigate a course without a chart,
To place your small hand in one larger still,
Is nothing less than very, very smart.
If satisfaction lags, just know you will
Be comforted in time and, patience is a skill.

LIFE'S LESSONS

PERSPECTIVE

Marcus Aurelius, an Emperor of long ago,
Advised his people one day:
"Live as though you lived on a mountain!"
(His idea of the very best way)

Mountain heights cause spirits to soar!
And take you above the daily grind.
The mountaintop person lives on an invisible peak
That exists solely in his mind.

His perspective is broad, his outlook far-reaching.
His spirit towers above the storms of life.
His mind is lifted up, above doubt and despair;
His vision is above the fog of petty strife.

The man with perspective has his head in the clouds,
But his feet are grounded in reason.
He keeps taking risks and daring the sky,
No matter what the season.

With perspective a person can dare to dream
And hold only good results in his mind.
Keep reaching, my dears, never give up your path,
No matter where it may wind.

THE SOURCE OF POWER

Just take a look around you
And study the Natural Way:
The light in the sky above you...
(From blue to dapple gray.)
The unfolding of your ideas...
(Just short of miracle-play!)
The emptiness of space... (What is
Beyond the Milky Way?)
The fullness of all life...
(Though sometimes in disarray.)
The behavior of Saints...
(Exemplary, I dare say.)

　　The events of Nature are potent!
　　There's hardly ever a quirk.
　　They always evolve in accordance
　　With how things work.

Imagine what would happen
If the processes were neurotic.
A lazy sky would flicker...
(The light would be spasmodic.)
Your thoughts would be irrational...
(You'd feel quite idiotic.)
Space could become agitated...
(And likely quite chaotic.)
Life would seem quite useless...
(At best, only episodic.)
The Saints you could not trust...
(They might become despotic.)

Potency comes from knowing
And acting according to
What is happening right now.
The rest is up to you.

EMPATHY

The practice of empathy makes you 'other centered,'
Enabling you to reach out to your mates.
Through creative power of your imagination
You project into another; fear abates.

While sympathy merely mirrors another's trouble,
Empathy discovers its source.
Empathy searches it out with the skill of insight
And removes it with a positive force.

Through empathy you can appreciate another's feelings;
And your judgment's not impaired by emotions.
You do not work with others in terms of your beliefs,
But in terms of what gives them their 'notions.'

Through empathy you can study any person you meet
That you wish to understand or learn from –
To seek inspiration from the gifted, the happy;
Or to build tools to help those who are numb.

Empathy helps to create harmony in the home.
Playing the other's role opens the door
To understanding and respecting his feelings,
Allowing a relationship that offers more.

Practicing the art of empathy will enlarge your world.
It will enter your understanding; hence, your life.
Empathy inspires tolerance, forgiveness and compassion,
And from daily living removes strife.

MASTERING NATURE WITH UNDERSTANDING

Some people are successful in mastering life
While others permit life to master them.
Those who are tossed around by the world
Are said to be part of their own problem.

There's a side of you who goes along for the ride,
Letting events happen around, and to, you.
But wait a minute, there's also a side
That knows exactly the right thing to do.

Once you understand your opposing forces,
You come to a knowledge of truth... with gains.
Are you controlled by, or are you controlling, your thoughts?
Passion can drive you, but let reason hold the reins.

FRIENDSHIP: BE A FRIEND, TOO

Kind sentiment is nice, it sounds quite good,
But sentiment alone is not enough.
Without kind deeds to support the words
The likelihood of true friendship is rough.

If you're lucky enough to have a friend
Whose words and actions correspond,
Then you are blessed because you have
A special unbreakable bond.

And if you are someone who returns in kind
This friendship of words and action,
Then you're someone who is in great demand;
You've reached mutual satisfaction.

POINT OF VIEW

Sometimes it is hard to shed your own point of view,
To let others' opinions and points of view enter.
Everyone takes the limits of his own field of vision
For the limits of the world. We are our own center.

But the most fatal illusion is the settled point of view,
Because life is growth and motion.
Stopped by a fixed point of view, the person "dies."
(This is stated without emotion.)

"If there's any one secret of success," says Henry Ford,
"It lies in the ability to be objective..."
And see from the other person's point of view,
As well as your own. It is perspective!!

A point of view can be a dangerous luxury
When substituted for insight and understanding.
You really never understand another person
Until you can see things from where he is standing.

We cling to our own point of view, as if
Everything depended on our being 'right.'
Our opinions have no permanence, they gradually pass away –
Like autumn and winter, like darkness and daylight.

A simple rule in dealing with a difficult person
Is to remember (before it all goes askew):
This person is striving to assert his superiority.
You must deal with him from that point of view.

Always respect another's opinion and point of view,
Even if shared with aggressiveness.
No point of view can ever be the last one,
Owing to the fact that all experience is process.

HARNESS THE POWER OF HOPE

It is often thought that hope is all we have,
A desperate hanging-on to wishful outcomes.
The expression often heard is 'Hope and Denial,'
When people are facing odds that are fearsome.

But hope is the only thing stronger than fear.
We don't give up; we don't run away.
If we can believe that tomorrow will be better,
We can bear the hardships presented today.

It's said that hope is like the sun.
This analogy may make you most curious.
As we journey toward it, it casts a shadow...
The shadow of our burden which is behind us.

Remember the three Grand Essentials to happiness
In this life as you go along your path
Are something to do, and something to love,
And something to hope for. Work the math.

TAKE TIME FOR MEDITATION

The mind gets so busy! My thoughts are jumbled!
I can't decide which way to turn first.
Does this happen to you? Is it driving you mad?
The times when this happens are the worst!

It just means you've strayed from your Spiritual Self;
You've let yourself and others block the path back.
Twenty minutes a day in quiet meditation
Can be helpful to getting back on track.

Yoga, too, is "active" meditation.
The poses are learned in right order.
You get a physical workout and a quieted mind…
A healthy combination, and furthermore…
You'll feel healthier and less stressed
Than you have felt before.
You'll be inspired with the results,
And keep going back for more.

EDUCATION

It's been said that a good education
Is your passport to a more meaningful life.
Though your lives may be filled with uncertainties,
With education you'll function with less strife.

Oprah Winfrey says, "Education is the key
To unlocking the world," (as you learn).
The knowledge you gain will give you perspective,
Understanding, and the power to discern.

If you develop a passion for learning
You will never cease to grow.
Anyone who stops learning is old,
No matter how much they know.

The purpose of education is to replace
An empty mind with one that's receptive.
You learn more every day if you pay attention;
With openness of mind, one is more perceptive.

Education is not the learning of facts,
But the training of the mind to think.
Tomorrow belongs to those who prepare today.
Knowledge is there at the font. Take a drink.

There's no guarantee that education will be easy.
Very little worth having is easy to acquire.
Education is not the filling of a pail...
No, education is the lighting of a fire.

FEELING SAFE

Feeling safe is not often a subject for discussion.
It's an emotion that's not always in the conscious mind.
When someone you know asks you how you are,
`I feel safe` is the most bizarre answer you could find.

`Safe` can be defined as being free from harm and hurt;
Both physically and emotionally, I hasten to say.
The world around us can seem quite confusing,
But a safe place is a sanctuary, out of harm's way.

There are many, many things which help us feel safe –
All probably different, when compared together –
And each of us has his or her favorite choice,
A go-to safe haven to avoid the bad weather.

A safe space can be any space, with one thing in common.
(To get there you probably don't need to go far.)
The space must nurture you – encourage and support –
And allow your feelings to be just what they are.

We all want love and we all want to feel safe.
We want to be wanted and cared for... protected.
We want to like ourselves and feel okay in the world.
We want to be loved and feel safe... connected.

PLANNING

If you aim at nothing, that's what you'll get —
That, and your attendant feeling glum;
Sorry for yourself, probably mad at the world.
It's a bloody waste of time, and inherently dumb!

As a man sets aims, he upgrades his standing.
(The principle applies to women, too.)
No one will acquire what he doesn't reach for.
Remember that in everything you do.

By aiming, you have a result in mind.
Use your time, gather strength and direct your quest.
With all the momentum for blazing your trail,
You have a better chance to do your best.

You're sure to go places you otherwise would not.
(There's achievement in purpose alone.)
Remember, only through purpose is fortune made.
Planning, or aiming, sets the tone.

PROBLEMS AS OPPORTUNITIES

The ordinary oscillation of being
Will carry you through times both good and not.
What seems the worst of all there is to bear
Will pass, and leave behind a tender spot.

The biggest risk of all is not the grief;
That's only life at it's low ebb.
The risk is holding back life's forward motion,
And getting further tangled in the web.

Our troubles allow us to build a strong foundation
On which to assemble our lives.
The lessons learned from solving problems
Give us the tools we need to thrive.

So please consider the problems you encounter
As opportunities to grow and excel.
Looked at this way, the anxious moments fade,
And you'll have great stories to tell!!

REPEAT THIS MANTRA

We become what we think about...
...all day long.

We believe what we tell ourselves...
...all day long.

Our lives take on aspects of what we say...
...all day long.

So fill your hearts with thoughts of love...
...and then become them.

So tell yourself only words of love...
...and then become them.

Accept yourself for the miracles you are...
...and then become them.

To yourself, say, "I love you with all of my heart...
...just as you are."

To yourself, say, "You're perfect in every way...
...just as you are."

To yourself, say, "You're deserving of love today...
...just as you are."

OBSTACLES

There are plenty of difficult obstacles in your path;
Do not allow yourself to become one of them.
A path without obstacles probably doesn't lead anywhere.
Make planning and solving a part of your stratagem.

Henry Ford said that obstacles are the things you see
When you take your eyes off your goal.
The challenges you face make your life interesting,
And overcoming them makes your life meaningful.

You can let obstacles in your life be stumbling blocks,
Or else they can be your stepping stones
To pursue your goals; to aim for success.
If success, a cheer! If you give up... only groans!

Obstacles are put in your way for good reason:
To strengthen you – your growth depends on them.
Obstacles are opportunities in disguise.
Call songs of joy for your success your anthem.

LIFE'S GIFTS

SERENITY

Life is a series of natural changes.
Resisting them only creates more sorrow.
Let things flow naturally forward for you
For a happier present and a serene tomorrow.

We can be serene in the midst of distress,
And, in turn, make others around us more tranquil.
Smiling at someone evokes a return smile,
And the air is instantly filled with goodwill.

Go in the direction of where you find peace.
Serenity is the guard that soothes your soul.
Balance in all things comes from balance within.
Saying "yes" to Existence can be your role.

Go within to find serenity, to find peace.
Nothing beats patience and honesty for recovery.
Underneath the chaos of everyday living
Serenity is patiently awaiting your discovery.

INSIDE OUT

The media grinds out clear and loud
For all of us to hear,
If we don't use a certain soap,
Then we should not stand near.

Or if we want to find a mate
Then we should look like models...
Tall and thin, with manes of hair
Colored from fancy bottles.

With ears just so and bodies of steel,
A sweet little turned up nose...
Is this possible for everyone?
Now, what do you suppose?

Perhaps the world would be more in balance
If we were to examine our aims,
Instead of being concerned about
The shape and size of our frames.

AUTHENTICITY

Living deeply requires a commitment
To be present in your body at all times,
With awareness of things all around you,
And inside you throughout your lifetime.

Listening to your body is one thing,
But moving into it and being present
Requires an extra awareness –
A losing of self-consciousness is evident.

In our society today dualistic thinking is practiced:
"Right or wrong," "good or evil," "us or them."
It divides us, allowing us to falsely believe
That we are "chosen," while "they" are condemned.

This dualism results in attack and banishment
Of everything it won't accept.
But remember, when we attack we feed the very thing
That we hoped to destroy. It is kept.

Engaging in the game of pursuing outward enemies
Feeds what we would destroy, to our chagrin.
Instead, concentrate on understanding your own
Conflicting energies you find within.

A lot of conflict you have in your life
Is a result of not living in alignment.
You're not remembering the age–old advice:
"Be true to yourself!" It's your assignment.

As you become more aligned with the truth
Of who you are (it is freeing),
The question of liking yourself goes away.
It becomes a natural state of being.

Authenticity is the alignment of head, heart, mouth and feet –
Thinking, feeling, saying and doing the same thing.
This builds trust, and friends love friends they can trust.
A soul made visible is a breath of spring.

POWER OF THOUGHTS

"As a single footstep will not make a path on the earth,
So a single thought will not make a pathway in the mind…"
Henry Thoreau said these most practical words
When considering the subject of the power of thoughts.
"To make a deep mental path we must think over and over
The kind of thoughts we wish to dominate our lives."

We are shaped by our thoughts, and so we become what we think.
We all hold the power to create our own ideal worlds.
And the silent power of our thoughts influences others,
Even at a distance. Mind is one as well as many.
Think of the universe as an intricate and very large cobweb,
And human minds are the spiders that run its pathways.

You are standing today exactly where your thoughts have brought you.
And you'll be living tomorrow just where your thoughts will take you.
If you are stressed, believe me, it's not your situation.
It's your thoughts. And only you have the power to change them.
Peace is a choice, and you can be peaceful right now.
Peace has nothing to do with other people's thoughts or actions.

You have more powers than you could ever dream of;
You can do things you never thought you could do.
Your subconscious mind controls the actions you take.
What you think about continually will eventually come true.
There are no limitations on what you can accomplish,
Except the limitations placed by your own mind.

BE HERE NOW

The past is past, kiss it goodbye;
The here is now, not tomorrow.
So live in your present indebtedness,
And you'll avoid a life of sorrow.

Do not have regrets for the past;
You know it cannot be undone.
Since tomorrow is only a contemplation,
You must live today. Make it fun.

REST

Rest is something we talk about doing,
But usually something gets in the way
Of being able to rest, and regroup
Before continuing on with our day.

Rest helps prevent the onset of illness
That develops through chronic tension and worrying.
We can clear our minds and begin to focus
On creative solutions to our questions still lingering.

Maya Angelou said, "Every person needs to take
A day away... to separate the past from the future..."
With no problems confronted, or solutions searched for –
Just withdrawing from our cares for a mind cure.

There is virtue in work and there is virtue in rest.
Use both and overlook neither... sometimes
The best thing to do is absolutely nothing.
Renewing energy through rest is a good pastime.

HIDDEN CHANGES TO TRANSITION

Extremely happy events can be
As stressful as the other kind –
A job you've landed, or a great new love,
Can take its toll on humankind.
It's hard to spot because of your joy.
It's the kind of stress you do not mind.

Another kind of stress might come
From the loss of a special relationship.
Perhaps someone you cared for moved away,
Or you broke up a special partnership;
Or a friend died, or you lost a pet,
And it narrowed your field of companionship.

Changes in content or quality of home life
Have major impact, and bring transition;
Things like getting married or having a child
Can certainly put things into juxtaposition.
Returning to school or moving out of town –
Though positive in the end – changes one's life condition.

Work or financial changes can be
Stressful beyond what one is aware;
Getting fired, or retiring, or changing jobs
Can sometimes be a veritable nightmare.
So can changes you can do nothing about,
Like inner company changes with no fanfare.

Personal change can take its toll —
A change of lifestyle or of address.
A sleep pattern change, or stopping alcohol
Can leave you experiencing some distress.
A setback, a recovery, it all has effect —
Even the experience of great success.

A 'spiritual awakening' or increased insight
Are occurrences which can change you in midstream;
A new self-image, more social awareness,
Or the rediscovery of a wonderful old dream —
The wordless nameless shifts in your life,
When things become different than what they seem.

Yes, change takes its toll; you must manage your stress,
For it can cause illness, both physical and mental.
If you handle it well, it will work for you.
And if not, it can become quite detrimental.
All of us have stress, both 'good' and 'bad' kinds —
The importance of its management is monumental.

SEEK THE SACRED

The mighty arches, the windows stained,
Holy figurines looking down from on high,
And tall marble columns of tremendous girth
Raise one's eyebrows upward to the sky.

The feeling of awe inspired by these structures
Can put distance between you and a Higher Power.
You can feel so small and unworthy before
A deity that lives in a tower.

The Sacred is to be found... simply... everywhere.
It's there for the finding when you seek.
It's in the smile of your grandfather's eyes;
It's in every word that you speak.

The mystics of old had no bold structures;
They had hills and valleys and towns;
They had family and friends and conversations…
They found the sacred in daily ups and downs.

And the way to say it in the words of Scorcese,
And with plain talk, it adds to the poem:
"You don't make up for your sins in church,
But on the streets and in your home."

VACATIONS

Vacations are medicine for the soul,
And usually require the need to vacate...
Travel is often the method to get away,
To reconnect with ourselves, and re-create.

The choices are many! So many places to go!
Find what brings you joy, and go there.
The world is a book, and if you don't travel
You have only one page to share.

Doing nothing brings everything into perspective.
Rediscover your passions, your purpose, and plus...
Why do we travel? Not to escape life,
But so that life will not escape us!

The word 'vacation' summarizes it all:
Resurrection, rebirth, reincarnation, and re-sprout.
A holiday turns people into themselves.
Of this fact, there is no doubt!

Wherever you go, go with all your heart.
The energy expended gains you more than you give.
The bottom line? The message here?
Do not work more than you live!

THE PAUSE THAT REFRESHES

When you pause to look at your life and take stock,
And you determine that it is not quite a cake walk;
When you think you've reached a stumbling block,
With some new ideas you need to unlock –

The Gods have come together to demonstrate
The hidden lessons when reaching stalemate.
Take a look at your life that is up-to-date.
Look for changes you can begin to orchestrate
To change your views. Your ideas will rotate,
And you'll come up with plans that exhilarate.

Sometimes when your life feels like poppycock,
And you'd rather hide behind a great big rock –
You slow down and find a four-leafed shamrock,
And you're happily taking a brand-new walk!

A CLOSING THOUGHT

POETRY

It's the revelation
Of a sensation
That the poet
(Wouldn't you know it)
Believes to be
Felt only interiorly
And personal to
The writer who
... writes it.

It's the interpretation
Of a sensation
That was fueled by
A poet's sigh
And believed to be
Shared mutually
And personal to
The lucky one who
... reads it.

ABOUT THE AUTHOR

Kathryn Carole Ellison is a former newspaper columnist
and journalist and, of course, a poet.

She lives near her children and stepchildren and their families in the
Pacific Northwest, and spends winters in the sunshine of Arizona.

You might find her on the golf course with friends, river rafting, traveling
the world, writing poems… or enjoying the Opera and the Symphony.

LATE BLOOMER

Our culture honors youth with all
It's unbridled effervescence.
We older ones sit back and nod
As if in acquiescence.

And when our confidence really gels
In early convalescence…
'We can't be getting old!' we cry,
'We're still struggling with adolescence!'

Acknowledgments

I have many people to thank...

First of all, my amazing children—Jon and Nicole LaFollette—for inspiring the writing of these poems in the first place. And for encouraging me to continue my writing, even though their wisdom and compassion surpass mine... and to my dear daughter-in-law and friend, Eva LaFollette, whose encouragement and interest are so appreciated.

My wonderful stepchildren, Debbie and John Bacon, Jeff and Sandy Ellison, and Tom and Sue Ellison who, with their children and grandchildren, continue to be a major part of my life; and are loved deeply by me. These poems are for you, too.

My good friends who have received a poem or two of mine in their Christmas cards these many years, for complimenting me on the messages in my poems. Your encouragement kept me writing and gave me the courage to publish.

To Kim Kiyosaki who introduced me to the right person to get the publishing process under way... Mona Gambetta with Brisance Books Group. I marvel at her experience and know-how to make these books happen.

To Amy Anderson, Sonya Kopetz, Kerri Kazarba Schneider, and Ingrid Pape-Sheldon, my very creative public relations team of experts, who have carried my story to the world.

And finally, to John B. Laughlin, a fellow traveler in life, who encourages me every day in the writing and publishing process. John, I love having you in my cheering section.

BOOKS OF LOVE
by Kathryn Carole Ellison

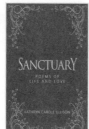